Woodland of Wonders

Survival of a Fawn

Kenzie Field

In the woodland of wonders,

the night becomes dawn.

In the long, blowing grass

lies a young forest fawn.

Now, this new baby deer
has been told he must wait,
to stay hidden and quiet,
while his mother ate.

This is called parking,
a new, valuable skill.
To protect him from harm,
he must stay very still.

The white spots on his back,

they will help him to blend.

He's disguised in the grass—

can you see our small friend?

His brave mom takes a sniff
with her sensitive snout.
She can smell if they're safe,
and no predators about.

His mom shows all is well
with a flick of her tail.
They start off on their walk
down the long, winding trail.

They must find all their friends,
and stay bundled together
for warmth and for strength
in this rainy, cold weather.

Lying next to his mom,
he observes her cupped ears.
As her brown eyes grow wide,
a strange movement appears.

The coyotes are hungry

and advance their prowl.

Sneaking through the tall grass,

they attack with a howl.

A quick, valiant buck
waves its furry white tail.
He is signalling danger –
fawns must run and not fail.

The brave deer use sharp hooves
and strong antlers to fight.
To defeat the coyote's
attacking, mean bite.

The fawn follows his mom
to ensure he's not prey.
He's been given directions
to run far away.

The scared fawn runs and runs,
fast as his legs can go.
To make sure he is safe,
there's no time to be slow.

The coyotes give up
and their pace starts to ease.
Without looking behind,
the deer rush to the trees.

The mom finds her tired fawn
and they share an embrace.
They're all fortunate deer,
not one lost in the chase.

The light turns to dusk,
and mom lies by her fawn.
As they snuggle up close,
he can't help but to yawn.

He is learning great skills
from his mom every day,
to escape and stay safe
'til he goes his own way.

Dedicated to

my son Beau

Inspired by my environmental science background,

and educating our little humans about our natural environment.

FIELD KITS Publishing

March 2024

Author

Kenzie Field

Editors

Kathryn Boucher & Jaimee Guenther

Illustrator

Canva AI

ISBN: 978-1-7383200-1-1

© All rights reserved. No part of this book may be reproduced in any form or by any electronic or mechanical means, including information storage and retrieval systems, without permission in writing from the publisher and copyright holder, except in the case of brief quotations embodied in critical articles and reviews. This is a work of creative nonfiction. Some parts have been fictionalized to varying degrees.

Woodland of Wonders Book Series

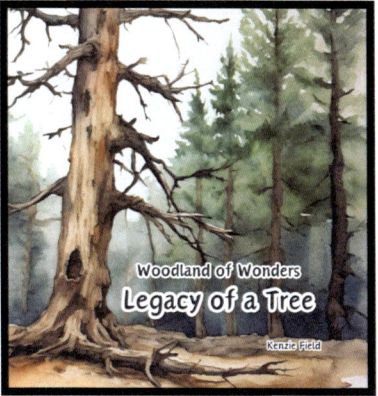

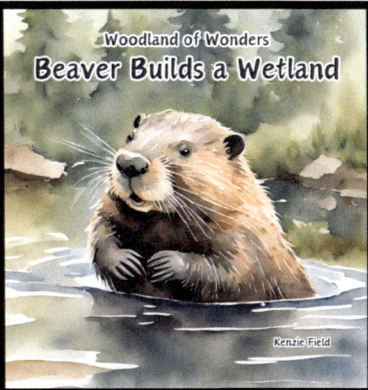

www.ingramcontent.com/pod-product-compliance
Lightning Source LLC
Chambersburg PA
CBRC091724070526
44585CB00009B/172